WREN'S *London*

COLIN AMERY

Lennard Publishing 1988

Lennard Publishing
a division of Lennard Books Ltd

Lennard House
92 Hastings Street
Luton, Beds LU1 5BH

British Library in Publication Data

Amery, Colin, 1944–
  Wren's London.
  1. (City) London. Buildings designed by
  Wren, Sir Christopher, 1632–1723.
  Architectural features
  I. Title
  720′.92′4

ISBN 1-85291-009-7

First published 1988
© Colin Amery 1988

Phototypeset in Bembo

Cover design by Pocknell and Co.

Printed and bound in England by Butler and Tanner Ltd, Frome.

CONTENTS

SIR CHRISTOPHER WREN

It all began in flames. Almost everyone knows of the meeting between King Charles II and Dr Christopher Wren only ten days after the Great Fire of London had broken out in September 1666. The thirty-four year old professor and scientist had, in a matter of days, prepared a scheme to present to his sovereign for the complete rebuilding of the burned City according to a regular plan.

Wren seized the initiative. He knew how important it was to be the first to present a plan. His friend John Evelyn was to offer his ideas for the city's future only three days later and at least two others were to follow, Professor Robert Hooke and Valentine Knight. None of these four gentlemen were what we would think of today as architects. They were much cleverer and more distinguished than anyone the organised profession has since produced. Architecture in the seventeenth century was not a profession but it was something that Wren and his intellectual equals would naturally understand and appreciate and any educated man would learn and understand the conventions of the Roman Orders and probably have read the standard Italian treatises. Wren's colleague John Evelyn considered architecture "the flower and crown as it were of all the sciences mathematical".

Wren had extraordinary mathematical talents and with a group of scientists who were later to form the hub of the Royal Society, he developed an experimental process of learning. Astronomy was Wren's chief interest early in his career and he made models that showed the periodic relationships of the sun, moon and earth. He had particular skills when it came to the making of models to demonstrate and test scientific theories. Inventiveness and an interest in geometry were later to facilitate his development as an architect.

There can be no doubting Wren's brilliance. In 1653 he was made a Fellow of All Souls studying science until 1657 and in that year he left Oxford to become the Professor of Astronomy at Gresham College in London. In 1661 he was back at Oxford as the Savilian Professor of Astronomy. At 29 his talents were described by Professor Robert Hooke; "there scarce ever met in one man, in so great a perfection, such a Mechanical Hand, and so Philosophical a Mind." He had demonstrated his interest in architecture by including in a scientific meeting in 1660 "new designs tending to strength, convenience and beauty in building." When he was asked by his uncle, the Bishop of Ely, to design the new chapel of Pembroke College, Cambridge in 1663, he was able to produce a highly competent, if not inspired, piece of text-book classical architecture. It was clearly derived from Serlio's *Architettura* and at the time was entirely new for the University where the Fellows Building at Christ's had been the most up to date piece of design. Wren's second building, the Sheldonian Theatre at Oxford, also followed in antique prototype. This time, a Roman theatre design was adapted ingeniously for the English climate by the addition of a flat ceiling. To our eyes today it is a curiously unsuccessful building – but in it are the seeds of his later inventiveness. Wren was to follow the Sheldonian by a modest building for Trinity College Oxford. At about the same time in 1665 he took his first and only trip abroad, to France, "to survey the most esteemed Fabricks of Paris."

The visit to Paris and the Ile de France were very much a preparation for Wren's subsequent work in London but he cannot have imagined the scope the Fire was to offer him. It was an important time for the arts in Paris where King Louis XIV and Cardinal Mazarin offered extraordinary patronage. He briefly met Gian Lorenzo Bernini to examine his designs for the Louvre, "but the old reserved Italian gave me but a few minutes view". However Wren went daily to watch the progress of the huge palace. He also particularly admired the baroque domes of Mansart and Lemercier's Church of the Val-de-Grace, and Lemercier's own design for the domed church of the Sorbonne. He would also have seen the now vanished church of Sainte Anne-la-Royale by the Italian Guarino Guarini and admired its structural originality. We know that Wren took enormous interest in the actual techniques of building and he was also intrigued by the engineering works of the quays along the Seine.

Wren's other sources of architectural knowledge would have come from the library, as well as the pioneering classical work, of Inigo Jones and his more immediate predecessors John Webb (1611–72) and Sir Roger Pratt (1620–85). We know that as a man of science he believed in the primacy of mathematics. In a lecture he gave in 1657 on the subject Wren explained that geometry and arithmetic are the keys to all other disciplines of thought because they are "void of all uncertainty". And yet in his architecture we can now see that Wren was interested in more than just mathematical certainty. He was interested in the imagination. He applied his imagination to the adaptation of the rules to produce buildings that are in themselves moving experiments in spatial and structural geometry. In London this imagination was to apply to his vision of, not just one great cathedral, but of a skyline for the whole new City.

Wren changed the whole face of London. A glance at a painting like Thomas Wyck's (1617–77) View of London, or Vischer's famous engraving of the City seen from Southwark in 1616, shows a crowded, spiky medieval skyline. The huge Gothic cathedral of old St Paul's (by 1616 without its spire) rises on the eminence to the west and the whole of the City to the east is a mass of towers and spires. Wren knew the power of that view from the south bank of the Thames and it is fascinating to think that one man transformed the Gothic dream city into an equally striking but rational and classical vision. Medieval London was not planned like some Italian cities – it had grown with a commercial pragmatism as it was to do again. The old city had also been the seedbed of the 1665 Great Plague and horrific though the Fire was, it purged London of timber buildings and gave Wren the opportunity to transform the city with brick and stone.

WREN'S PLAN

Wren produced a plan that was Utopian and impossible to carry out. On paper it looks abstract and too much like the solution to a problem of geometry. From London Bridge four streets radiate reaching at their northern extremeties four main northern gates of the City. The widest street led to the Royal Exchange; which seems to sit at the centre of an angular spiders web of radiating streets. The fixed points of the perimeter of the plan were the city gates, the bridge and the two main public monumental presences in the city – the Royal Exchange and the cathedral. Along the river a quay forty feet wide ran from the Tower to the Temple Garden. The street pattern ignored the existing haphazard jumble and imposed a grid, with as many street corners as possible being right angles. There were some wonderful features of the plan which ignored all proprietorships and could only have been achieved under an absolutist regime. Taking the plan from west to east – after crossing the widened Fleet River (now a canal in the Dutch style with wide quays) an arch of triumph in honour of the king as the founder of the New London marked the foot of Ludgate Hill. The hill rising up to the cathedral was to have been almost one hundred feet wide. At the cathedral the road split into two – one branch to go to Tower Hill and another to the Royal Exchange. The Royal Exchange with double porticoes stood in a wide Forum surrounded by great new buildings for the Excise, Mint and the Goldsmiths. New churches were to be built at selected sites where they articulated streets or ended vistas. Many of them were to be freestanding. They were to be designed, "according to the best forms for capacity and hearing, adorned with useful porticos, and lofty ornamental towers and steeples in the greater parishes."

London's survival, at a time when an expensive war against France and the States General was being prosecuted, depended upon commerce and this meant immediate reconstruction. A rebuilding commission was announced in October 1666 – Wren, Hugh May, and Roger Pratt appointed Commissioners by the King; and Robert Hooke, Peter Mills and John Oliver nominated by the City. They were charged with a responsibility to survey the damaged City and to consider how best it should be rebuilt. They drafted the Rebuilding Act of 1667 but it was to take some forty five years before Wren's new skyline was to be substantially complete. The first Act forbade half-timbered buildings and any new buildings were to be almost standardised and built of brick and stone to the satisfaction of building inspectors. There was to be a second Rebuilding Act in 1670, and it was not until after that date that work was to begin in earnest upon Wren's fifty two City churches. Work was not to start upon the building of St Paul's Cathedral until 1675.

Wren's speedy submission of a plan for the new city had secured him a key seat on the planning Commission and by 1669 he was in an unassailable position, being appointed Surveyor of the King's Works – a post he was to hold for the next fifty years. Wren was the most powerful architectural figure in the Kingdom and it was on London more than anywhere that he was to leave his mark.

WREN'S CITY

It seems a long way from the simple Renaissance classicism of Wren's early churches in London to the spire of St Vedast, one that seems to be inspired by Borromini. This is because they mark the evolution of his style. The City churches were begun in the 1670s but often their towers were not begun until the 1690s and thus it is possible to see the development of Wren as a designer. While many of the churches show ingenuity in their plans it is the steeples that demonstrate Wren's unparalleled architectural assurance.

The rebuilding of the fifty two City churches constitutes the greatest accomplishment of Wren's career. With St Paul's they represented a consummate achievement of European architectural significance. There is no doubt either that the loss of so many of the churches by official vandalism, war and ecclesiastical philistinism is the greatest loss sustained by London. It is heart breaking to compare the panoramas of London's skyline in this book and watch the creeping destruction of Wren's work. The Victorian architect A.H. Mackmurdo loved the City churches and he saw that the point of them was that the whole parade of them was so much greater than the individual parts. Writing in 1883, he observed that

" . . . this characteristic of unity in design is then the first and most important of these City Churches, a characteristic which gives to London an interest above that enjoyed by any Continental town . . . from the tower of St Saviours' Southwark, the entire group is to be seen, and I know of no more magnificent sight . . . this view of London, wrapt in her day-dark halo earth cloud . . . the pale cathedral lifting itself aloft – a miracle of unmoved dignity, boldly central among her square massive mansions, and huge blocks of seven-storied offices; its dome as soft in outline, as tender in graduated light, as any summer cloud, yet standing not alone, but surrounded by her daughter churches, whose steeples blazon the sky with pinnacles of sable and silver – a most lovely sight. . . . We look upon all these churches as so intimately connected with one another, that St Paul's bereft of its surrounding steeples, is to us as a parent bereft of her children – a Niobe in architecture."

How did Wren, the scientific genius and newly fledged architect, achieve such unity of design and impose such clarity of vision upon the City? It is easy to underestimate Wren's political, as well as his architectural, achievement. He had the support of the King, but he still had to convince humble parishes as well as powerful merchant interests to accept the new architecture. It is hard to imagine one man, even a genius like Wren, having the same success and powerful impact on the City after the bomb damage of the Second World War. It says a lot for oligarchy – the influence of a small group of like minded and learned men undiluted by bureaucracy who enjoyed powerful support at Court. They were, under Wren's leadership, able to provide England with a classical architecture that was distinctive and original.

One of the main reasons for Wren's success was his pragmatism. His churches and even his palaces at Greenwich and Hampton Court all show that he was able to compromise. To have been able to accept the rejection of the Great Model design for St Paul's and to continue to work with a clergy that did not understand classicism shows a flexibility and lack of arrogance rare in great architects. That is not to say that Wren's pragmatic English baroque is a weak compromise – it is strongly individual and varied. It was the architecture of possibility, and Wren discarded almost as many schemes as he built and looking at his rejected designs it can be seen that he learned as he progressed. His work does not have the passionate intensity of a Borromini. Wren was a rational scientist – a great constructor who turned to the art of architecture. He was not a sculptor or painter, like Bernini, but he was prepared to experiment and invent. If St Paul's is flawed as a totality it is because it reflects Anglican compromise, but at the same time possesses Wren's virtues of freedom and experiment. Better a flawed Christopher Wren than a stale Palladian copy.

London's City churches are the key to Wren's development as an architect. There was a certain luck in the timing of Wren's commissions. The City churches coincided with his decision to concentrate on architecture and the delay in the starting of St Paul's meant that he was able to apply the lessons and experience provided by the churches. They are the key to his cathedral because on them he learned the lessons of spatial planning and the ingenious use of difficult sites. Classical interiors had to be squeezed on to the angular and awkward sites of the Middle Ages and medieval spires tranformed into a completely new classical equivalent. It was a massive task. Eighty seven churches were destroyed in the Great Fire. The second Rebuilding Act of 1670 increased the tax on coal shipped to London and much of it was to be spent on the churches and the remainder on St Paul's cathedral. With parish amalgamations it was decided to rebuild fifty two churches. A small committee was established – Wren, with Dr Robert Hooke and Edward Woodroffe seem to have been the prime movers.

It is difficult to acquire an accurate picture of Wren's exact intentions when it comes to the City churches. Clearly he intended to enshrine the medieval memory of a city of spires and steeples in the classical language of his time. When it comes to the interiors his intentions have been masked, changed and in many cases lost or ruined by speculative post war restoration. Imagine a stone coloured classical room with high wooden pews and some panelled wainscotting flooded with the light of reason from clear glass windows. The clarity and dignity of this space would have been enriched by carved and gilded wood. In most cases, this vision is denied us. On the outside of his churches, Wren was reusing the old, cramped sites and he had little opportunity to build grand façades. Compared to seventeenth-century churches on the Continent, London's contemporary churches are, apart from their towers and spires, almost invisible and certainly less memorable. Nonetheless, because of the use of stone in a predominantly brick city, Wren's churches had a dignifying effect on the street.

OPPOSITE St Paul's seen through the ruins of St Mary-le-Bow.

There are two main types of church designed by Wren. One was the large rectangular plan divided into traditional nave and aisles. In St Bride, one of the sixteen churches started in 1670, arcades divided the nave and aisles – the arches of the arcade carried on coupled columns. Like any Vitruvian basilica, all of Wren's large churches have five bays. St Bride has a high plastered barrel vault with clerestory windows, oval in form, cutting into the vault. It is all very Venetian and the east end of the large churches often experiment with scaled up versions of the Venetian window. St Bride, in its restoration has been much altered, as indeed has St Mary-le-Bow. The plan of St Mary-le-Bow is quite an unusual one because of the site. Only the large tower fronts on to Cheapside where the entrance is – and the congregation had to turn left to face the east end in a wide three bay church. Here Wren separates nave and aisle by piers with half columns, a device taken from the Basilica of Maxentius in Rome. The lost church of Christ Church Newgate Street probably had the best interior of the larger churches (1677). Giant Corinthian columns are set on high bases, keeping the gallery away as an integral but secondary space while the ceiling had shallow and beautiful cross vaults making incorporation of the clerestory much simpler. Outside the City at both St James's Piccadilly and St Clement Danes Wren creatively varies his interior solutions.

The other type was the centralized church. Wren was very interested in the centralized plan for some of the church sites. Making the square meet the rectangle was a test of the imagination and often produced the shallow dome. St Mildred Bread Street, now destroyed, was a good example with barrel vaults at the east and west ends and a central dome. St Swithin Cannon Street, also now destroyed, had an eight sided dome over the main area and both St Benet Fink and St Antholin had oval domes. Some churches, like St Martin Ludgate, St Mary at Hill and St Anne and St Agnes have an inner square at the centre of the church defined by four columns. This rather Dutch treatment – the cross in the square – has a great similarity to Haarlem's Nieuwe Kerk.

But it is at St Stephen Walbrook that Wren's spatial ingenuity is most consummately expressed. Here on the plan the cross in the square meets the central dome. This is an extremely complex church. The wood and plaster dome rests on eight equal arches carried on twelve columns which form a square. Cool, clever, balanced and ingenious Wren has reached the ideal he was seeking in this interior. The almost rough plasterwork of the dome and the curious insertion of a centrally placed Henry Moore travertine altar give the church a strange quality that is almost secular. St Stephen represents the synthesis of so many of Wren's ideas and achieves the perfect merging of the longitudinal building with the central plan type.

Some of the geometric complexity that is found in Wren's planning is to be found in three dimensions in his steeples and towers. Stone and lead are the two materials used and they were often added to earlier churches as late as 1700 when London was again prosperous. The early example of St Mary-le-Bow is however as formally exciting as any of the later ones. At 225 feet high above the balustrade of the square tower everything changes to a circular spire that is two small columned temples topped by a soaring pyramid supporting a dragon weather vane. This was the first many storeyed classical steeple in England, and it was probably based upon engravings of Antonio de Sangallo's model for St Peter's in Rome. Others are equally compelling. St Bride has diminishing octagons, St Vedast Borromini – like curves, Christ Church Newgate Street is almost Neo-classically Ionic. The simpler lead spires are equally inventive, but it is the west towers of St Paul's cathedral

OPPOSITE The still burning ruins of Christ Church, Newgate Street, 1941.

that are the culmination of Wren's study of the Roman baroque – a study he made from contemporary engravings.

Crucial though they were to London and, as the photographs in this book show, vital to the skyline, the fate of the City churches has not been a happy one. Only four of the fifty two churches had vanished by 1850. In 1854, because the residential population was moving to the suburbs the Bishop of London drew up a list of twenty nine churches he proposed to demolish. This list included, St Peter Cornhill, St Mary Abchurch, St Mildred Bread Street, St Mary Aldermary, All Hallows Lombard Street and St Alban Wood Street. The Times of the day called it a 'vast act of desecration' and public protest saved some of the churches. The Union of Benefices Act of 1860 was however passed by Parliament, and fourteen churches were sold and destroyed by 1888. Eight more went after that date. The mid-Victorian climate of medieval ecclesiology which loved Gothic must have been partly to blame. Neither Pugin nor Ruskin had much time for Wren. But our century has been equally careless. In 1926 the guardians of the churches, acting upon the Phillimore Report of 1919, proposed the demolition of nineteen churches, not all by Wren but including St Magnus, St Vedast, and St Mary at Hill. This time there was a fervent public outcry objecting strongly to this Anglican philistinism. But although only one church was to go under this measure, the Second World War damaged or destroyed some twenty churches of all periods in the City. As a result, some of the churches we see today, like St Lawrence Jewry, St Mary-le-Bow, St Vedast or St Bride are Wren outside but so much altered inside that they are scarcely Wren churches.

St Paul's is the reason for the churches – the cathedral presided visibly in the past over her great brood of children. Enough has been written about Wren's greatest building but it bears repeating to say that it is the perfect English marriage between the classical and the baroque. The dome is the most restful composition in the world. The west front with its double portico of coupled, Louvre-like columns and its twin Roman baroque towers is now so familiar that it is hard to appreciate its intense originality. Wren would undoubtedly have preferred the completely centralized Great Model version, but it says a lot for his patience and skill that he achieved the architecturally impossible and married the Gothic nave to the domed classical conception. This is not the work of a dogmatist. The cathedral speaks of tolerance of plan and form, and it is that workable tolerance that is at the heart of Wren's work. Spatially glorious, inside the cathedral shows a balance between carved detail and massive scale that is perfect.

For London as a whole St Paul's should *still* be a crucial focus. The view of it from the Thames escorted by its procession of steeples was one of the wonders of Europe. War and Mammon have deprived us of that view for ever. Even the view of London from Wren's own Greenwich is as I write about to be horribly ruined by the commercialization of London's Dockland by the Canary Wharf development. This will include a 900 feet high tower of unspeakable banality. Closer in to the City there seems no good reason why the offending top stories of Faraday House on Queen Victoria Street should not be lopped off to return the view of St Paul's to those looking from the south bank of the Thames – especially from Blackfriars Bridge. It is too late to plead for the creation of the great river quay that Wren planned from the Temple to the Tower – but how that would have helped London and the Thames.

But there is still a major second chance to do something about the immediate surroundings of St Paul's. In 1987 a developer held an international competition for the Paternoster site to the north east of the cathedral. It is an area ripe for renewal. Lord Holford's plan of the 1950s – apparently picturesque on paper – was an architectural disaster. There is a glorious second chance to rebuild the entire area. Unfortunately the developers competition did not produce a very impressive result. The

An impression of the intended development at Canary Wharf, looking west over the City.

seven architectural firms (Arata Isosaki from Japan, Skidmore Owings and Merrill from the United States and five British firms – James Stirling; Norman Foster; Richard Rogers; Arup Associates; and Richard MacCormac) were all asked to produce a master plan for the area. The winner was Arup Associates but who were invited to develop their ideas. During the summer of 1988 they exhibited their very preliminary thoughts and were joined in the exhibition in the crypt of the cathedral by another scheme produced by John Simpson, which responded to the Prince of Wales's speech at the Mansion House in 1987, when the Prince had begged for more beautiful buildings around the cathedral. HRH The Prince of Wales called for more effort to be made to design sympathetically close to our great monuments like St Paul's. The Simpson proposals are classical in style and propose a network of brick buildings that are of a human scale well detailed and appropriate to the cathedral.

None of the entries to the Paternoster competition seemed to be aware of the importance of Wren. That is one of the reasons for this book. Perhaps a glance at some of these photographs will show how beautiful London was and underline how little recent generations have respected it. The second chance is now – with a building boom in the capital a strong public desire for a return to order and humanity in architecture.

What has Wren to offer to architects today? The answers are simple and eternal ones. Wren created an English tradition by following the more tenuous lead of Inigo Jones. He had a fine and accurate mathematician's mind that saw the potential for classicism in England. But he did not slavishly copy the Italian masters – he applied their language but remained original and inventive not capitulating to any style. When Wren was reporting on the project to build the City churches he wrote that – 'plainess and durability ought principally, if not wholly to be studied.' Simple but valuable lessons. Wren understood the profile of buildings against the English sky. This is something that has been totally lost. You are lucky today if you get a service tower on a building – why not pinnacles, domes, spires? Wren too had a sense of the appropriateness of detail and he understood how to win the support of his craftsmen. Not just wonders like Grinling Gibbons but bricklayers and lock makers and lead masters and everyday joiners.

Wren the scientist and model maker understood the craft of building. Today Wren would have accepted and used the girder, the concrete beam and reinforcement. But he would not have tolerated false materials. He would have made his models to see how the increased available spans effected the scale of his works. He would have built tall but not out of scale with city. He would have put functionalism in its place and brought back gracefulness to building. It is impossible to overestimate Wren because he did not see the problem architecture in isolation from his scientific training. He brought art reason and science together in a way that was quite remarkable. His particular genius combined with opportunity gave London an architecture which is hard to define. I would suggest that it is an especially English kind of eloquence. The design of a building combined with detail and quality of the worked materials is something that is purely Wren. Sir Edwin Lutyens understood it and indeed produced his own version which he called 'Wrenaissance'. A glance at Lutyens's little Midland Bank next to Wren's St James's Piccadilly shows this almost undefinable quality in both buildings. Wren's other superb gift – and it is one that has been cruelly destroyed in London – was his capacity to see architecture in relation to the city as a whole. Although his plan for London was not built it influenced the thinking and profile of what was built. Sir Edwin Lutyens writing in *The Times* in 1932 to mark Wren's Tercentenary summed it up.

"Wren lived in a period of transition. He was faced with a debris of a medieval civilisation. The spirit of compromise was abroad. He had to face difficulties which to a less gifted man would have been insuperable. Yet he succeeded in impressing his personality not only on his fellow workers and craftsmen but on the buildings he erected during the reign of four kings. He imparted to eighteenth-century architecture the very fibre of its being. It is this humane quality, this regard for graceful expression apart from style, which is the basis of his life's work. For my own part I view the work of Sir Christopher Wren as a beacon which never fails to inspire. And there is no finer monument to his genius than the character he gave to London."

It is time that Wren's spirit inspired the future surroundings of his cathedral. St Paul's stands in a sea of mediocrity, almost drowning. How can we let the second millenium pass without an attempt to learn again from Wren and make his City glorious again. It is almost too late. His own plan for a colonnaded piazza (developed by Hawksmoor) with a splendid baptistery in front of the west end of the cathedral would be the perfect starting point. The terrible irony of the fate of the City skyline and the surroundings of St Paul's is that if they had been in East Germany they would have been restored and treated as the serious works of art that they are. London has been harsh to Christopher Wren – at least around St Paul's it is not too late to begin some atonement. These photographs show the glory there was. The flames burned again in the Blitz – can Wren's phoenix rise again?

CASUALTIES BEFORE THE ERA OF PHOTOGRAPHY

It was Charles Dickens in his book *The Uncommercial Traveller*, who took a look at the City churches in the 1850s. He thought then that he had more knowledge of the churches of Rome than of those in his own city of London, but he nonetheless painted a stark picture of desertion and decay which marked the beginning of the transfer of congregations from the old city to the suburbs. The City Fathers had from the early 1830s attempted the reduction of the number of churches – St Michael Crooked Lane, St Benet Fink and St Bartholomew-by-the-Exchange had gone by 1840. They hoped to demolish a further 13 that they considered superfluous. However the news that they would be expected to replace them with new churches in the suburbs soon discouraged them. It was left to the church itself to speed up the process of architectural decimation. Following the passing in 1860 of the Union of City Benefices Act some 22 churches were disposed of – 16 of which were Wren's. After the First World War, Bishop Winnington-Ingram appointed a Commission that recommended the demolition of a further 19 churches at one go. There was, at length, much protest. Thomas Carlyle, supported by William Morris, Sir George Gilbert Scott, George Edmund Street and Holman Hunt, wrote to the City Churches and Churchyard Protection Society . . .' that it would be a sordid, nay, sinful piece of barbarism to do other than preserve these churches as precious heirlooms, Many of them are specimens of noble architecture, the like of which we have no prospect of ever being able to produce again.' By the end of the Second World War there was much loss and damage but from 47 churches in 1939 there are now 39 in use and restored.

ST CHRISTOPHER-LE-STOCKS. Wren's repairs and alterations to a medieval church culminated in the gothic tower of 1712. All was demolished in the 1780s. *OPPOSITE.* ST MICHAEL CROOKED LANE, 1684–98. A most distinctive church, demolished in 1831 to make a new approach to London Bridge.

St MICHAEL'S CHURCH CROOKED LANE
taken on the spot the day before the Workmen
began taking down the Vestry Room, for the
approach to the new London Bridge

TOP LEFT. ST BENET GRACECHURCH STREET 1681–7. Destroyed 1876. *TOP RIGHT.* ST OLAVE OLD JEWRY, 1670–6. Demolished 1888–9. *BOTTOM LEFT* ST MICHAEL BASSISHAW 1676–9. Demolished as late as 1900. *BOTTOM RIGHT* ST BENET FINK. Another ingenious, polygonal church, destroyed in 1846.

TOP LEFT ALL HALLOWS, BREAD STREET, 1677–84. Demolished in 1876 to make way for warehouses. *TOP RIGHT* ST GEORGE BOTOLPH LANE, 1671–9. Demolished 1903–4. *BOTTOM LEFT* ST MARY SOMERSET, 1686–94. All but the tower was destroyed in 1870. *BOTTOM RIGHT* ST MARY MAGDALEN, OLD FISH STREET, 1683–7. Destroyed by fire in 1886.

TOP LEFT ST ANTHOLIN, WATLING STREET, 1680–6. The loss of this highly original church was an astonishing act of vandalism. *TOP RIGHT* ST ANTHOLIN. The interior was an elongated octagon, resting on Corinthian colums. *BOTTOM LEFT* ST MILDRED POULTRY 1670–7. Demolished in 1872. *BOTTOM RIGHT* ALL HALLOWS THE GREAT, 1677–82. Demolished 1876–94.

ST BARTHOLOMEW EXCHANGE, 1674–81. This church was destroyed in 1841.

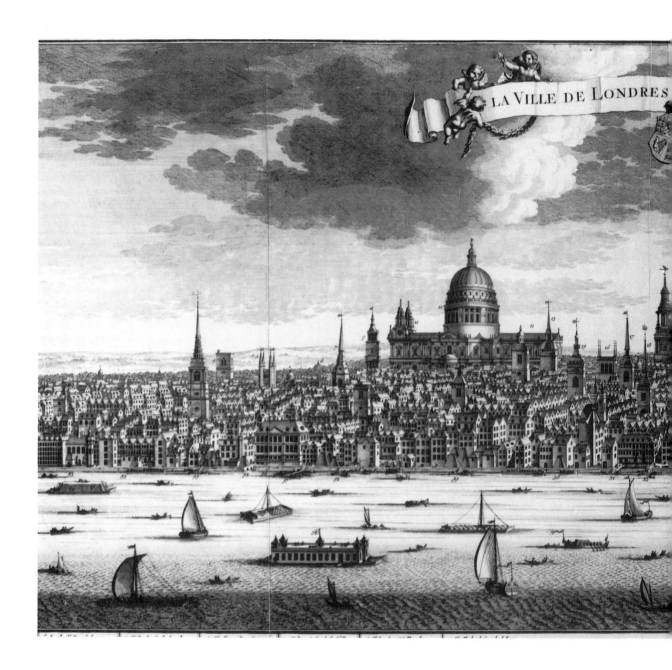

A prospect of London of 1710 that shows St. Paul's and all Wren's City churches soon after they were built. As A. H. Mackmurdo wrote in 1883 – 'Without breaking the bounds of architectural propriety, or disgracing dignity of form, Wren has given us, in his fifty three churches, as many varieties of steeple outline . . . The result of calm choice of individual

form, combined with severe discipline in imaginative composition, shows itself in each one of these masterpieces of architectural design.' And more than that, as this view shows, Wren saw the whole of the City as an architectural composition – the cathedral is the culmination of the procession of churches.

1753 A mid-eighteenth-century view from the northern heights of London before the great expansion of the major estates.

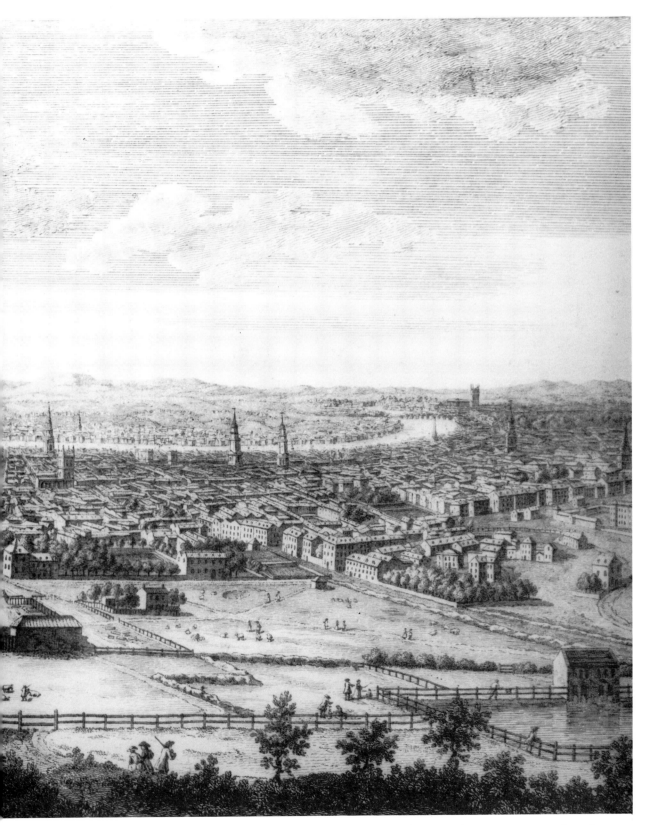

The great height of St Paul's, 365 feet, is particularly striking in this view seen against the
Surrey hills.

London circa 1859. A gloriously romantic view of the stone and lead spires and the cathedral rising above the workaday brick world of the trading city. The tallest spire (right foreground) is St Michael Queenhithe, demolished in 1876. The tower furthest to the left is

St Mary Somerset. The working riverside has today been replaced by car parks roads and ill designed buildings that obscure what remains of Wren's vision. The photograph is a calotype from the fourth volume of the Prince Consort's collection.

View *c*. 1850 from St Bride's, Fleet Street. Even with the rise of commerce and the smoking chimneys, Wren's vision of London's skyline triumphs.

1930 and 1960: Views from St Brides.

Two views from Point Hill, Blackheath, South East of St Paul's, 1951 and 1981.

1921 Aerial view of Southwark and Cannon Street.

1895 – 6 Birds's eye view from the tower of St Mary-le-Bow. Although Cheapside and the monster Cannon Street Station are Victorian and many Georgian buildings have been replaced, the skyline is still much as Wren intended.

WEST OF ST PAUL'S

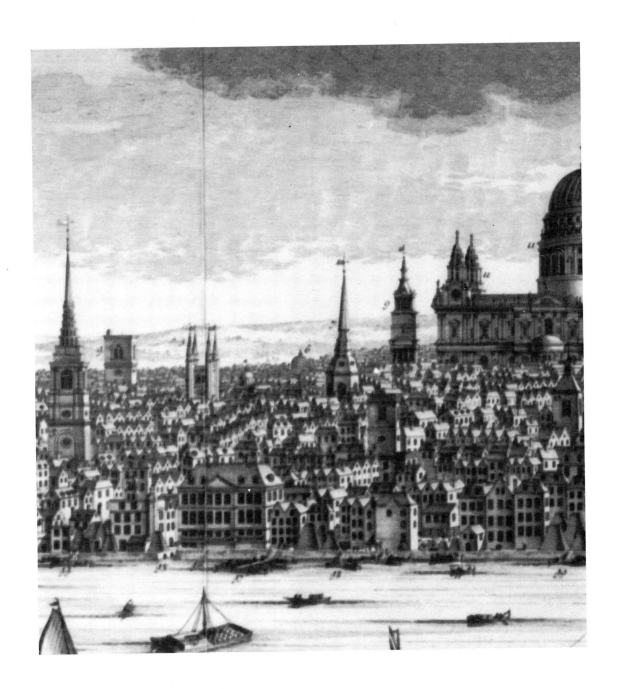

ST BRIDES, 1671–1703. Gutted in 1940, restored by Godfrey Allen and reopened in 1957. To see it surrounded by eighteenth-century houses shows the scale of the wedding cake spire to have been even more magnificent, delicate and ingenious than is possible to see today.

ST BRIDES. Another view of the steeple in harmony with the buildings around it, before their destruction in the Blitz.

ST BRIDES. The collegiate plan of the arcaded interior is modern as is the imitation of Wren's Hampton Court reredos. The original feeling of a great room full of dark oak, carving and candles has been lost. This is that older interior, photographed c 1930.

ST BRIDES. A detail of the urns that adorn the steeple.

North Side of St Andrew's Holborn (1866).

ST ANDREW HOLBORN, 1684–92. It escaped the Fire of London but was rebuilt
nonetheless. Here shown as it was in 1866, burned in 1941, it was reopened in 1961. Its
strange and elaborate tower with complex windows and urns resting upon Roman altars is
perhaps its finest feature.

ST ANDREW HOLBORN. The interior is remarkable for the six light Venetian East
window and gilded encrustations of the plasterwork. The restoration, by Lord Mottistone
of Seely and Paget, is well done.

ST MARTIN LUDGATE, 1677–87. Its slender lead spire, casually encircled by a viewing gallery for looking up Ludgate Hill to St Paul's, is one of Wren's best. How well it gives scale to the cathedral and demonstrates the way Wren thought of the whole of the City as an artistic composition.

ST MARTIN LUDGATE. The square, domed interior is still conservatively treated, the later lowering of the pews making the Corinthian columns more impressive.

ST ANDREW BY THE WARDROBE, 1685–95. Late Wren at his most simple and clear.

Photographed in 1870, with St Paul's behind it, the church seems well sited and at ease.

ST ANDREW BY THE WARDROBE. The interior, as restored by Marshall Sisson in 1961 is perfect for its restraint and dignity. Hard now to imagine the church overwhelmed by followers of the passionate preacher William Romaine (1766–95) but the simple power of the architecture remains. It is also Wren at his most styleless, simply designing what was modestly appropriate.

CHRIST CHURCH NEWGATE STREET, 1677–87. Once one of Wren's largest church interiors and full of the noise and life of the Bluecoat boys from neighbouring (until 1902) Christ's Hospital School. The tower and some of the walls survive (tower by Wren, 1704) but the present City Corporation demonstrated their love of Wren by demolishing walls that had survived the Blitz for road widening.

CHRIST CHURCH NEWGATE STREET. Note the elegant geometry of the diminishing
squares of the tower, decorated by urns. The photograph dates from 1904.

ST BENET PAUL'S WHARF, 1667–83. A cheery brick and stone cube, garlanded with carved swags of fruit and flowers.

ST BENET PAUL'S WHARF. Undamaged by the Second World War the interior remains a business-like example of Wren's work. Corinthian pilasters and columns define the spaces and all is neat and ordered.

ST BENET PAUL'S WHARF. In 1970, some of its surroundings still survived.

ST PAUL'S from the Thames – a calotype of 1854.

AIRE & CALDER
BOTTLE WAREHOUSE

HORSE SHOE WHARF

OVERLEAF ST PAUL'S dominates its surroundings as it was intended to do.

ST PAUL'S. Christ Church Newgate Street – the tower is seen here without the twelve urns which were removed in 1814 but restored by a private benefaction in 1959. Wren clearly considered the squareness of this tower in relation to his dome.

ST PAUL'S. St Paul's Churchyard by the South Transept.

ST PAUL'S. From the west – St Martin Ludgate Hill on the left.

ST PAUL'S. From the east – St Vedast Foster Lane to the right.

ST PAUL'S. From the East – spires from the left St Stephen Walbrook, St Mary Aldermary (Gothic), St Mary-le-Bow.

ST PAUL'S. From the East – still an even roofscape in the City.

ST MARY MAGDALEN OLD FISH STREET, 1685. A fire of 1886 led to the ruin and final destruction of this church which was most remarkable for its stone lantern rising on five octagonal steps above the tower parapet. The interior was famous for its notable fittings but only a few tablets and the font survive in other churches.

ST MARY MAGDALEN OLD FISH STREET. The interior following the fire of 1886.

ST AUGUSTINE WATLING STREET, 1680–96. In his *City Churches* Mackmurdo wrote, "when walking up the old approach to St Paul's – Watling Street – we see Wren has so placed the steeple of St Augustine, that its sharp terminal may prick the yielding clouds, immediately in front of St Paul's circling vault."

ST AUGUSTINE WATLING STREET. The interior, which was completely destroyed in the war. It had been, however, considerably altered from Wren's original, as this view of 1909 shows.

ST NICHOLAS COLE ABBEY, 1671–81. Always considered to be the first church rebuilt by Wren after the Great Fire, it was burned out in 1941, restored by Arthur Bailey and reconsecrated in 1962.

ST NICHOLAS COLE ABBEY. Chandeliers, carving and decorative treatment once made this a model City church interior. Today it has suffered from too drastic restoration and unsuitable stained glass. Photographed before destruction in the Blitz.

ST MARY SOMERSET, 1686–94. Today is is hard to imagine this tower and its church as part of a coherent street. How well it looked – before the traffic and road widening ravished Upper and Lower Thames Street – superbly in scale with the tall warehouses, incredibly glamorous with its obelisks against the sky and very swanky alongside St Benet's seen to the west. The interior was very plain. All but the tower was demolished in 1871.

ALL HALLOWS BREAD STREET, 1680–1684. A tower incorporated into a simple rectangular plan – this was one of Wren's simple rooms with a flat ceiling and lots of light from plain glass arched windows. It went as early as 1876 to allow for more warehouses in the City. Its fine pulpit found its way to St Vedast Foster Lane and the organ front to St Mary Abchurch.

ALL HALLOWS BREAD STREET. Interior looking east, photographed before 1876.

ST MILDRED BREAD STREET, 1682. Bombed in 1941, the 140 feet elegance of this slender lead spire – like a stretched obelisk topped by a crown – is one of the great losses of the City.

ST MILDRED BREAD STREET. It was undoubtedly one of the best of Wren's interiors. Two deep coffered arches spanned the width of this small church creating a square from which sprang a beautiful small dome. Wren used the variety of his City churches to experiment, and there is no reason to doubt that this tiny essay had St. Paul's in mind.

ST VEDAST, 1670–97. The tower (photographed in the 1930s) demonstrates how well
Wren fitted his splendours into the texture of the everyday City. More undulating and
Baroque than many, this tower in stone plays an important part in many of the views of St
Paul's. Today it just succeeds in triumphing over ugly and out-of-scale neighbours.

ST VEDAST. Inside the furnishings have been altered to make the church feel like a college chapel.

ST ANNE AND ST AGNES, 1676–81. The small church dwarfed even by late nineteenth-
century offices.

ST ANNE AND ST AGNES. The interior, *c*.1900.

ST MICHAEL QUEENHITHE, 1676–7 One of the casualties of the Union of City
Benefices Act of 1860 the church was demolished in 1876. It was a very grand exterior. But
the star item on top of the lead covered spire was the ship in full sail, the weather vane. This
survives on top of the church of St Nicholas Cole Abbey. Wren knew how to bring his
churches right to the street – giving a sense of architectural majesty that is almost Roman.

ST MICHAEL QUEENHITHE Showing its relationship with its surroundings. Photographed c.1870.

ST ALBAN WOOD STREET, 1682–87. In 1940 the church burned and today only the tower remains, recently converted into a house. Gothic in the hands of Wren has a powerful quality – there is almost a foreshadowing here of Hawksmoor's Westminster Abbey towers.

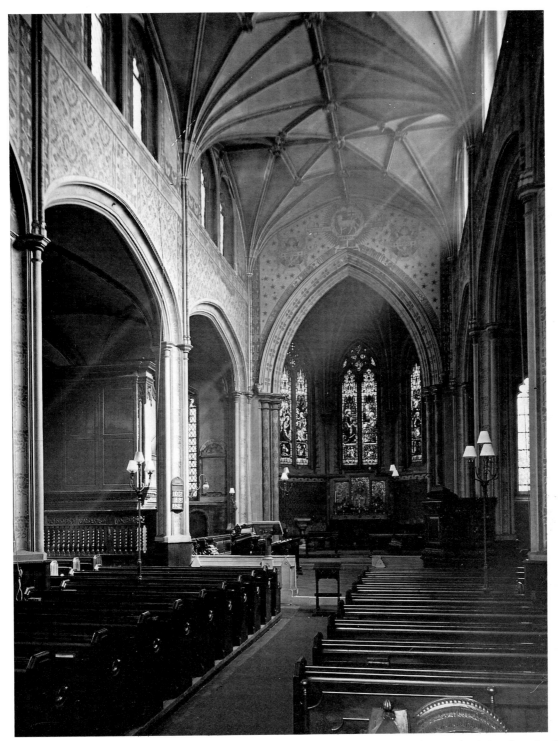

ST ALBAN WOOD STREET. Much of the church suffered under the Gothicizing hand of Sir George Gilbert Scott as can be seen from his apsed treatment of the East end (1858).

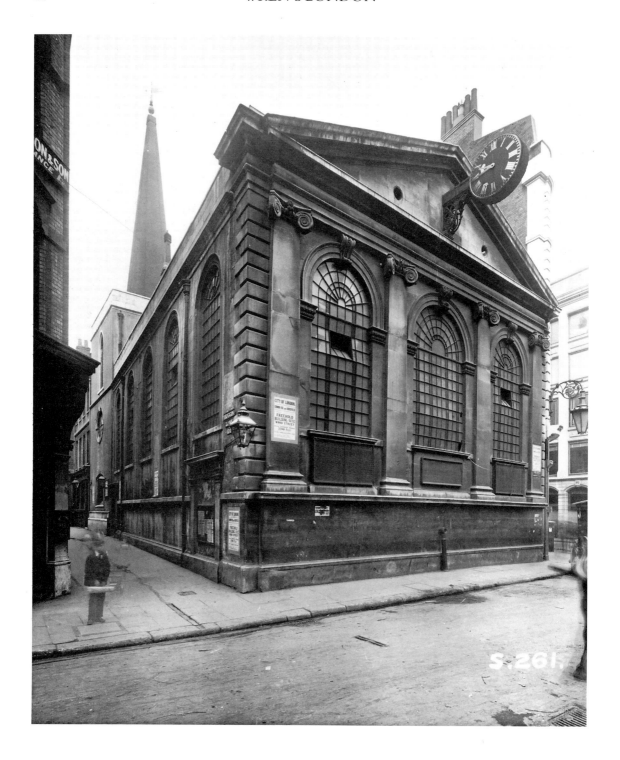

ST MICHAEL WOOD STREET, 1670–5. Another church sold in 1894 as a freehold building site (see notice on pilaster) when its parish was united with St Alban Wood Street.

ST MICHAEL WOOD STREET. It had been much altered inside during the nineteenth century and was full of pseudo Gothic deal furniture. The east end (shown here) had a good civic presence.

ST MARY-LE-BOW, 1670–80. This church was burned in 1940. Wren's grandest stone
spire is the home of the famous Bow Bells, but should be admired for its architectural
complexity and geometrical resolution. The way that the tower projects into Cheapside is a
brilliant stroke of townscape design.

ST MARY-LE-BOW: as it was. The interior of the church was completely remodelled by Laurence King "on contemporary liturgical lines" in the 1960s and it is tasteless and devoid of the spirit of Wren.

ST MARY-LE-BOW, in ruins in 1946, six years after war damage.

ST MARY-LE-BOW. The sophisticated doorway, photographed in 1946.

ST MARY ALDERMARY, 1679–1682. Wren goes Gothic to suit the remaining tower and the wishes of the donor. Photographed in 1870.

ST MARY ALDERMARY. Inside the shallow domes are made to look like fan vaulting, and it is hard to feel that the eighteenth-century Gothick has not already arrived. Suitably high church with the most redolent incense in the City. *OVERLEAF. ST MARY ALDERMARY*, detail of plaster vaulting.

ST JAMES GARLICKHYTHE, 1676–83. Nakedly exposed by the widening of Thames Street, Wren's ingenuity in fitting his lantern-like church onto its site is now rather wasted.

ST JAMES GARLICKHYTHE. The Portland stone steeple on the tower is very comely and by far the most elaborate thing about this plain church.

ST JAMES GARLICKHYTHE. Wainscot and plaster dominate the inside, restored by David Lockhart-Smith in a way that looks successfully old.

ST JAMES GARLICKHYTHE. A detail of the walling taken in the 1850s.

ST MARY ALDERMANBURY, 1672–87. This church is the only Wren church to have been transported across the Atlantic. To commemorate Anglo–American collaboration in the Second World War, and to mark the spot where Sir Winston Churchill made his Iron Curtain speech, this church was rebuilt at Westminster College, Fulton, Missouri. Its site in London has been excavated.

ST MARY ALDERMANBURY. The results of bombing. *OVERLEAF.* ST MARY
ALDERMANBURY in its old home between the wars.

ST LAWRENCE JEWRY. This photograph of the vestry shows why it was often described as London's loveliest room, till its destruction in the Blitz.

ST LAWRENCE JEWRY, 1670–87. There is more than a smack of St Paul's about the east end of this church with its carved swags and blind niches (*SHOWN OVERLEAF*). As the church of the Lord Mayor and Corporation it has a certain municipal splendour. Completely destroyed in 1940 the restoration by Cecil Brown is sumptuous but not in the darkly rich old way.

ST MICHAEL BASSISHAW, 1676–9. The strange dedication was simply a corruption of
St. Michael of Basing's Hall and the church stood close to the Guildhall on Basinghall
Street. Wren replaced the burned medieval church by a grand tunnel-vaulted new church
with a tower and spire rising to some 140 feet.

ST MICHAEL BASSISHAW, the interior. Work to clear the crypt of human remains revealed weak foundations and the church had to be demolished in 1899 when the parish was incorporated with St. Lawrence Jewry.

ST ANTHOLIN, 1678–87. There is no chance that you will hear one of the famous 5 am sermons here as the Victorians destroyed this church in 1874. The stone spire seen here partly survives in the garden of the Forest Hill Social Club. However that is no substitute for the octagonal plan which gave the church such a striking interior.

ST MICHAEL PATERNOSTER ROYAL, 1686–94. The church is shown here before severe damage in World War II. Not restored after bomb damage until 1968, it is now the headquarters of the Mission to Seamen.

ST MICHAEL PATERNOSTER ROYAL. It was restored by architect Elidir Davies, with modern glass by John Hayward to commemorate Dick Whittington who was buried here. More interesting outside than in, the modern work has removed all sense of Wren – his solid Cityness so well caught in this photograph of 1920. *OVERLEAF.* ST MILDRED POULTRY, 1670–7. On the right before its destruction in 1872.

ST OLAVE OLD JEWRY, 1670–6. Sold for the greater glory of Stoke Newington in the 1880s when Victorian missionary zeal moved to the suburbs, today only the tower remains. Part of the tower houses an agreeable rectory for the combined parish with St Margaret Lothbury. To enter offices through the former church doors feels like a victory for mammon.

ST OLAVE OLD JEWRY. The sale of the church, ignominiously displayed in this photograph from the 1880s.

ST STEPHEN COLEMAN STREET, 1674–6. A pleasing pineapple on a pediment and a
straight sided spire end this City vista.

ST STEPHEN COLEMAN STREET. Inside, beneath the flat ceiling, there was a rare long, low reredos and a finely carved communion rail. Austerity rather suited a church that replaced one where communion was once only given to those considered virtuous by a parish committee. Obliterated by enemy action in 1940.

ALL HALLOWS THE GREAT, 1677–82. Standing on Upper Thames Street, All Hallows must have been impressive for its massive qualities, and the unusual placing of the tower at the east end of the north aisle. Wren built it in 1683 but it had a chequered later history. Its tower and north aisle were moved in 1876 to allow Queen Victoria Street to be widened.

ALL HALLOWS THE GREAT, a detail of the interior before demolition in the 1870s. Under the Union of City Benefices Act the church disappeared, and the site was sold to a brewery. The tower which remained was bombed in 1939 and the final indignity was the erection of the appalling Mondial House on its site in 1969.

ST STEPHEN WALBROOK, 1672–77. One of the greatest of Wren's churches – arches, circles, columns, all conspire to raise up the coffered central dome. Godfrey Allan skilfully restored the war damage but his discretion has been overcome by placing under the dome a carved altar by Henry Moore. The church was described as "a compromise between the austerities of Calvinism and the splendours of Baroque Rome."

ST STEPHEN WALBROOK. The exterior showing the relationship of the steeple and dome. *OVERLEAF.* ST STEPHEN WALBROOK. Interior.

ST MARGARET LOTHBURY, 1686–93. How Italian Lothbury looked when lined by classical stone banks that respected the scale of Wren's church. His tower carries a very successful lead spire that today finds it hard to compete with the rise and rise of the office block.

ST MARGARET LOTHBURY. Inside, this particular church has become something of a repository for the furnishings of the churches that the Victorians demolished and so it is doubly rich.

ST SWITHIN CANNON STREET, 1677–81. Wren was clever here – he planned a square that turned into an octagon and then became a dome. To carry everything through he gave the church an octagonal spire. Photographed *c.* 1865.

ST SWITHIN CANNON STREET, The interior was spoiled in 1869 when unsuitable windows were inserted, in contrast to the previous view. The steeple was described by the architect Mackmurdo as "grim and strange" – it is a loss to the skyline. The ruined church was finally demolished in 1962, following bomb damage in the Second World War.

ST CLEMENT EASTCHEAP, 1683–87. There is something modest and unpretentious about this place that survives even the recent enthusiastic gilding. It is another classic Wren oblong box, tucked away but worth finding for the good English plasterwork and the interesting but unsuitable altarpiece by Ninian Comper.

ST CLEMENT EASTCHEAP. The interior.

ST MARY ABCHURCH, 1681–86. Wren makes magic here, magic somehow enhanced by the fact that the church is even more dwarfed and hidden away than he would ever have expected.

ST MARY ABCHURCH. Because you step directly from the quiet brick exterior into the square church the circular shallow painted dome comes as a glorious surprise. Apart from the dome there is an authenticated Grinling Gibbons oak and limewood reredos – the king of carvers.

ST EDMUND KING AND MARTYR, 1670–76. Only probably by Wren, this church may well be the work of Wren's surveyor Robert Hooke. Better from the outside than in, it adds considerably to Lombard Street, with its good tower and lead steeple centralised on the entrance front. This shows the east end.

ST EDMUND KING AND MARTYR. A very plain interior. *OVERLEAF.* ST EDMUND KING AND MARTYR. In Lombard Street, *c.* 1900.

ALL HALLOWS LOMBARD STREET, 1684–94. The last of Wren's City churches to be completed, it closed in 1937 when it was demolished to allow for the building of the new head office of Barclays Bank. Always deeply concealed from view by the towers of banking it was known as 'The Church Invisible'.

ALL HALLOWS LOMBARD STREET. The entrance.

ST MICHAEL CORNHILL. Although Wren made the plan, the tower is by Nicholas Hawksmoor. It certainly demonstrates his power as a three dimensional designer and pays substantial homage to the soaring pinnacles of King's College Cambridge. This church was heavily Victorianised by Sir George Gilbert Scott.

THE CHURCHES IN THE EAST

ST PETER CORNHILL, 1677–85. The Key of St Peter is poised on top of the tall lead spire above the brick tower. The rest of the exterior is modest, stucco and brick and pleasingly hidden away among plane trees.

ST MAGNUS MARTYR. The church is one of Wren's noblest interiors – two rows of great fluted columns carry the unbroken entablature – and everything is still white and gold.

ST MAGNUS MARTYR. *c.* 1900

ST BENET GRACECHURCH STREET, 1681–7. One of Wren's ingeniously simple plans – the tower and the vestry and church were all within a rectangle. Inside the lofty interior was lit by a double bank of high windows illuminating the painted red and gold curtains of the reredos. The tower and lead steeple were remarkable combining dome, lantern and obelisk. Demolished for road widening in 1867.

ST GEORGE, BOTOLPH LANE, 1670–7. One of the very first churches to be rebuilt by Wren after the Fire. For speed and economy he utilised the rubble from old St. Paul's cathedral.

ST GEORGE BOTOLPH LANE. The street frontage of the church which was demolished 1903.

ST MARY-AT-HILL, 1670–95. The east end, with its classical elements, harmonizes with its street.

ST MARY-AT-HILL. The west end, which was rebuilt in the late eighteenth century.
Surprisingly, this is a view of 1962.

ST MARGARET PATTENS, 1684–89. This church spire above the tall and thin tower is
still important in City views.

ST MARGARET PATTENS. Some of the original furnishings survive, like the Church-warden's canopied pews. Sadly the interior has been marred by the twentieth-century "improvements".

ST DIONIS BACKCHURCH STREET, 1670–84. A view of *c.* 1870. Once rather beautifully surrounded by little shops and houses the church had a strong square stone tower and its east end was flush with Lime Street.

ST DIONIS BACKCHURCH STREET. A victim of the vandalistic Union of City Benfices Act, this church with its peaceful churchyard was lost in 1878.

ST DIONIS BACKCHURCH STREET, the churchyard *c.* 1865.

ST DIONIS BACKCHURCH STREET. Two views of the interior, destroyed in 1878.

ST DUNSTAN-IN-THE-EAST. Probably not by Wren, this church was repaired and restored twice in the late seventeenth century. Only the tower and spire now survive.

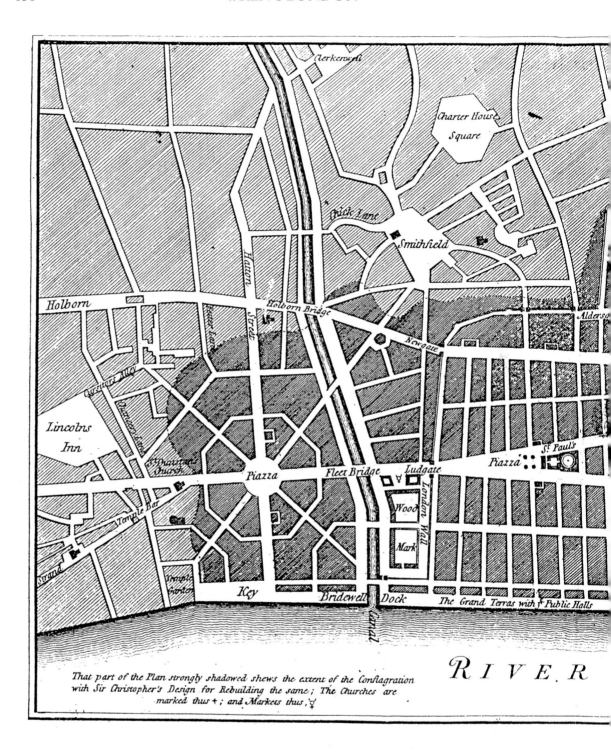

Wren's intended plan for London. This involved a complete redefinition of the street plan. It had piazzas, squares and wide streets, but it was bedevilled by the need to rebuild the City almost immediately.

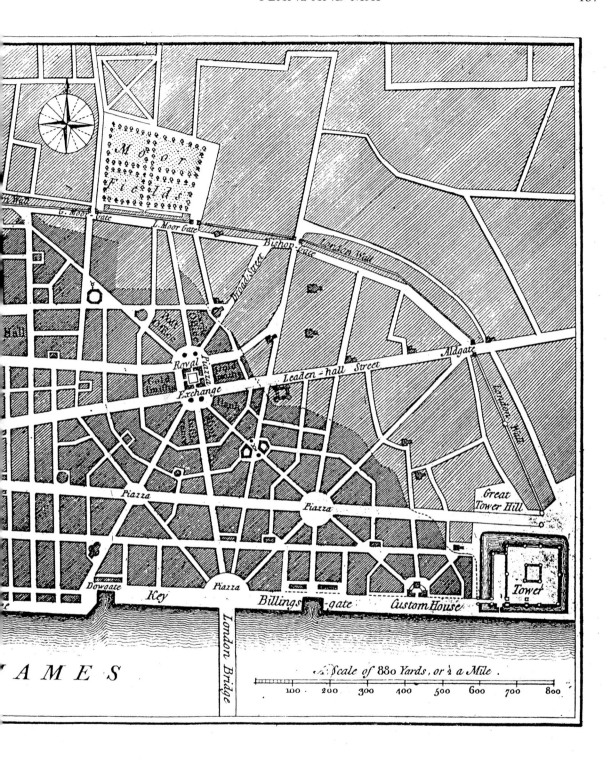

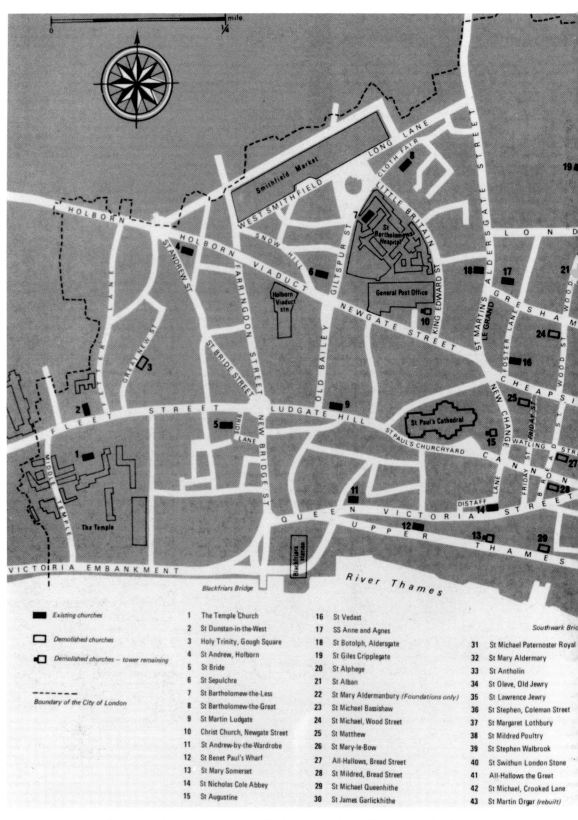

■ Existing churches		
▢ Demolished churches		
◪ Demolished churches – tower remaining		
- - - - - Boundary of the City of London		

1 The Temple Church	16 St Vedast	
2 St Dunstan-in-the-West	17 SS Anne and Agnes	
3 Holy Trinity, Gough Square	18 St Botolph, Aldersgate	
4 St Andrew, Holborn	19 St Giles Cripplegate	31 St Michael Paternoster Royal
5 St Bride	20 St Alphege	32 St Mary Aldermary
6 St Sepulchre	21 St Alban	33 St Antholin
7 St Bartholomew-the-Less	22 St Mary Aldermanbury (Foundations only)	34 St Olave, Old Jewry
8 St Bartholomew-the-Great	23 St Michael Bassishaw	35 St Lawrence Jewry
9 St Martin Ludgate	24 St Michael, Wood Street	36 St Stephen, Coleman Street
10 Christ Church, Newgate Street	25 St Matthew	37 St Margaret Lothbury
11 St Andrew-by-the-Wardrobe	26 St Mary-le-Bow	38 St Mildred Poultry
12 St Benet Paul's Wharf	27 All-Hallows, Bread Street	39 St Stephen Walbrook
13 St Mary Somerset	28 St Mildred, Bread Street	40 St Swithun London Stone
14 St Nicholas Cole Abbey	29 St Michael Queenhithe	41 All-Hallows the Great
15 St Augustine	30 St James Garlickhithe	42 St Michael, Crooked Lane
		43 St Martin Orgar (rebuilt)

London today showing the location of City churches, Wren's and others.

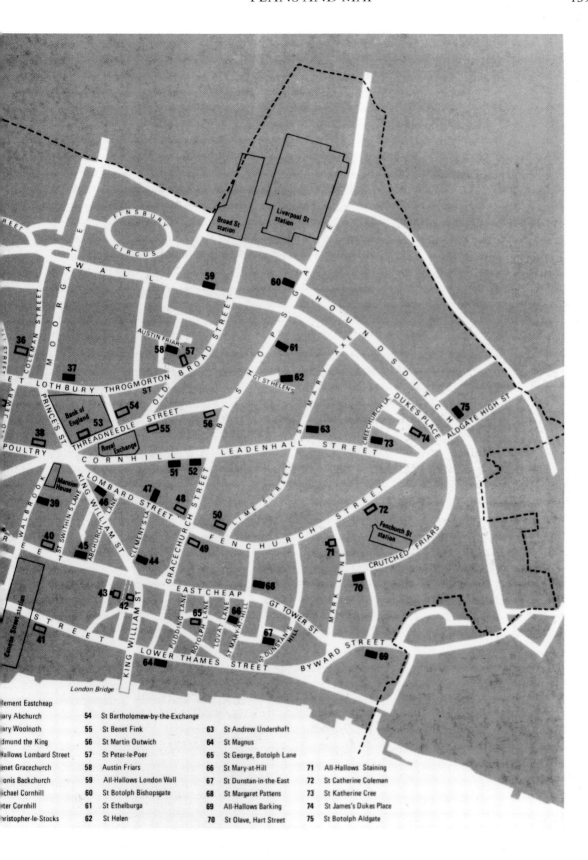

		54	St Bartholomew-by-the-Exchange				
lement Eastcheap							
ary Abchurch		55	St Benet Fink	63	St Andrew Undershaft		
ary Woolnoth		56	St Martin Outwich	64	St Magnus		
dmund the King		57	St Peter-le-Poer	65	St George, Botolph Lane		
allows Lombard Street		58	Austin Friars	66	St Mary-at-Hill	71	All-Hallows Staining
enet Gracechurch		59	All-Hallows London Wall	67	St Dunstan-in-the-East	72	St Catherine Coleman
onis Backchurch		60	St Botolph Bishopsgate	68	St Margaret Pattens	73	St Katherine Cree
ichael Cornhill		61	St Ethelburga	69	All-Hallows Barking	74	St James's Dukes Place
ter Cornhill		62	St Helen	70	St Olave, Hart Street	75	St Botolph Aldgate
hristopher-le-Stocks							

INDEX

ACKNOWLEDGEMENTS

The Publisher is grateful to the following for the material used in this book:-

The Guildhall Library: 10, 15, 16, 18, 19, 20, 21, 22–23, 24–25, 26–27, 28–29, 90, 100–101, 111, 123, 124.
Times Newspapers: 30–31, 32–33.
Greater London Records Office: 34.
Royal Commission on the Historical Monuments of England: 9, 17, 36, 37, 38, 39, 40, 41, 42, 43, 44–45, 46, 47, 48, 49, 50, 52, 53, 54, 56, 57, 58, 60, 61, 62, 63, 64, 65, 66, 68, 69, 70, 71, 72, 73, 74, 75, 76, 77, 78, 79, 80, 81, 82, 83, 84, 85, 86, 87, 88–89, 91, 92, 93, 94, 95, 98, 102, 103, 104, 106, 107, 108, 109, 110, 112, 113, 114, 115, 116, 117, 118–119, 120, 121, 122, 125, 126, 127, 128, 129, 130–131, 132, 133, 134, 135, 136, 138, 139, 140, 141, 142, 143, 144, 145, 146, 147, 148, 149, 150, 151, 152, 153, 154, 155.
Map of City churches from London City Churches by Gerald Cobb.